FIRST NATIONS OF NORTH AMERICA

NORTHEAST INDIANS

CHRISTIN DITCHFIELD

HEINEMANN LIBRARY
CHICAGO, ILLINOIS

www.heinemannraintree.com
Visit our website to find out
more information about
Heinemann-Raintree books.

To order:

☎ Phone 888-454-2279
💻 Visit www.heinemannraintree.com
to browse our catalog and order online.

Original illustrations © Capstone Global Library, Ltd.
Illustrated by Mapping Specialists, Ltd.
Originated by Capstone Global Library, Ltd.
Printed in China by China Translation and Printing Services

15 14 13 12
10 9 8 7 6 5 4 3

Library of Congress Cataloging-in-Publication Data
Ditchfield, Christin.
   Northeast Indians / Christin Ditchfield.
      p. cm.—(First Nations of North America)
   Includes bibliographical references and index.
   ISBN 978-1-4329-4948-8 (hc)—ISBN 978-1-4329-4959-4
(pb) 1. Indians of North America—Northeastern States—
Juvenile literature. I. Title.
   E78.E2D57 2012
   974.004'97—dc22   2010040612

Acknowledgements

The author and publisher are grateful to the following
for permission to reproduce copyright material: Bentley
Historical Library: p. 34 (University of Michigan); Corbis:
p. 14 (Nativestock Pictures/© Marilyn Angel Wynn); Getty
Images: pp. 5 (Nativestock.com/© Marilyn Angel Wynn), 20,
29 (Nativestock.com/© Marilyn Angel Wynn), 31, 33 (MPI),
38 (Bill Frakes /Sports Illustrated), 41 (PAUL J. RICHARDS/
Staff); Library of Congress Prints and Photographs Division:
pp. 4, 11, 19, 30, 35, 37; Lin Photo Art: p. 26 (Linda Ross);
Nativestock Pictures: pp. 13 (© Marilyn Angel Wynn), 16 (©
Marilyn Angel Wynn), 18 (© Marilyn Angel Wynn), 21 (©
Marilyn Angel Wynn), 22 (© Marilyn Angel Wynn), 27 (©
Marilyn Angel Wynn), 28 (© Marilyn Angel Wynn), 32 (©
Marilyn Angel Wynn), 39 (© Marilyn Angel Wynn), 40 (©
Marilyn Angel Wynn); Shutterstock: pp. 12 (© Doug Lemke),
25 (© nialat); The Granger Collection: pp. 15, 17, 24, 36.

Cover photo of a carved wooden Seneca False Face "Scalp
Mask", used in rituals by the Seneca peoples of New York,
reproduced with permission The Granger Collection, NYC.

We would like to thank Dr. Scott Stevens for his invaluable
help in the preparation of this book.

Every effort has been made to contact copyright holders of
any material reproduced in this book. Any omissions will
be rectified in subsequent printings if notice is given to
the publisher.

All the Internet addresses (URLs) given in this book were valid
at the time of going to press. However, due to the dynamic
nature of the Internet, some addresses may have changed, or
sites may have changed or ceased to exist since publication.
While the author and publisher regret any inconvenience this
may cause readers, no responsibility for any such changes can
be accepted by either the author or the publisher.

Contents

Some words are shown in bold **like this**. You can find out what they mean by looking in the glossary.

Who Were the First People in North America?

When the people of Europe first came to live in North America, they thought they had discovered a "New World." They didn't realize that this New World was already **inhabited** by millions of people, belonging to as many as 500 different **nations**. There are at least 3 million **descendants** of these first peoples still living in North America today.

▶ This man is an Ojibwe Indian.

Native American or American Indian?

In 1492 Christopher Columbus became the first European explorer to reach North America. He thought he had arrived in the Indies (South Asia), so he called the people he met "Indians." Although it soon became clear that Columbus had landed on a different **continent**, the people he encountered there continued to be called "Indians" for centuries.

In the 1960s, some people began expressing their dislike for the name "Indian." Some people said they should be known as Native Americans. (A native is a person who was born in a particular place.) Others preferred to be called American Indians, Natives, or First Peoples. Today all of these names are used to describe the race of people who have lived on the North American continent longer than anyone else. However, most of these people prefer to be called by their **tribe** or nation name, such as Iroquois or Onondaga.

▲ This Menominee girl is a fancy shawl dancer performing at a special celebration of her tribal heritage.

How Did People First Come to North America?

Scientists believe that the first people to come to the North American **continent** came across land that connected North America to Asia. This is called the land bridge theory.

The land bridge theory

The Bering Strait is a waterway that runs between Russia and Alaska. Scientists believe it may once have been dry land, or that the water may have frozen during the **Ice Age**. Sometime around 10,000 BCE, people from Asia walked across this land bridge from one continent to another. They may have been hunting, following large herds of animals. They may have been looking for a new land with a better climate or more **natural resources**. These people and their **descendants** soon spread throughout North America, Central America, and eventually South America.

STORIES AND LEGENDS

Creation Stories

Northeast Indians have many stories and legends about how their people came to live on the land. According to one story, a Sky Woman fell to Earth and was caught by a giant sea turtle. Other sea creatures helped the turtle pile mud on his back to create a huge island (North America) as a place for the woman and her children to live. In another story, the All-Maker created the world and filled it with people to enjoy its beauty.

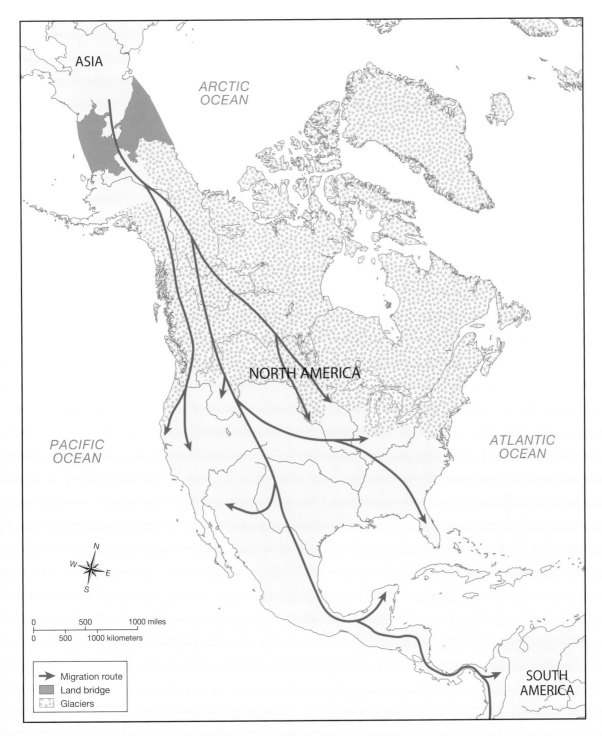

ASIA

ARCTIC
OCEAN

NORTH AMERICA

PACIFIC
OCEAN

ATLANTIC
OCEAN

N
W   E
S

0   500   1000 miles
0   500   1000 kilometers

→ Migration route
▨ Land bridge
⋯ Glaciers

SOUTH
AMERICA

▲ This map shows how the first humans may have come to the Americas.

Tribes and nations

As the first people spread out across North America, they traveled in **clans**, or family groups. Several clans living and working together formed **tribes**. Joining together with other tribes, they became **nations**.

Although at one time they were all related to each other, the tribes and nations living in different regions developed their own unique **characteristics**. They adapted, or changed, their way of life to fit their surroundings. They created their own languages, their own religious beliefs, and their own **culture** and **customs**. Each tribe's culture, or way of life, was different from the culture of other tribes. However, tribes that lived near each other tended to be more alike than tribes living thousands of miles apart.

Anthropologists (scientists who study people groups) have identified ten distinct groups of American Indians—Arctic, California, Great Basin, Northeast (sometimes called Eastern Woodland), Northwest Coast, Plains, Plateau, Southwest, and Subarctic. Each of these groups is made up of many smaller, individual groups that share a similar way of life. This book is about the Northeast Indians.

LANGUAGE

Family Trees

One of the ways that anthropologists can tell which tribes are most closely related to each other is by studying their languages. Tribes that speak the same language or nearly the same language have probably come from the same part of the country. They most likely have common **ancestors** and come from the same family tree.

ARCTIC
OCEAN

PACIFIC
OCEAN

ATLANTIC
OCEAN

Arctic

Subarctic

NORTH
AMERICA

Northwest
Coast

Plateau

Great Basin

Plains

Northeast

California

Southeast

Southwest

Gulf of Mexico

N
W   E
S

| 0 | 500 | 1000 miles |
| 0 | 500 | 1000 kilometers |

▲ This map shows the different regions in which groups of American Indians share similar characteristics.

Who Are the Northeast Indians?

There were once as many as 50 individual American Indian **tribes** living in the northeastern part of what is now the United States and southeastern part of what is now Canada. Some lived near the Great Lakes, such as the Ojibwe, the Menominee, and the Potawatomi. Others lived along the coast of the Atlantic Ocean, from Nova Scotia to North Carolina. These included the Wampanoag, the Narragansett, and the tribes of the Powhatan **Confederacy**. Still others lived in the region that is now the state of New York and Ontario, Canada. These included the Huron, the Erie, and the Iroquois Confederacy.

◄ The Northeast Indians are also known as Eastern Woodland Indians, because the area in which they lived had many trees and forests.

Getting along with other tribes

Many Northeast Indian tribes lived at peace with one another. Members of one tribe married members of another. Their families remained closely related. Some tribes even formed confederacies. They formally declared themselves to be allies and friends. Other tribes were fierce enemies, often at war.

Hiawatha

According to an Iroquois myth, Hiawatha was an Onondaga warrior. His wife and children were killed by another tribe. Hiawatha chose not to seek revenge. Instead he traveled throughout the Iroquois territory with a message he received from a **prophet** called the Peacemaker. Hiawatha called on the Iroquois people to follow the **Great Law** and live together in peace.

▲ This illustration shows one depiction of the legend of Hiawatha.

What Is the Northeast Like?

American Indian communities that lived in the Northeast adapted their way of life to both the climate and the **terrain**. The climate of the region varies.

▲ The Northeast region has many forests, mountains, and lakes such as the ones seen in this photograph of Eagle Lake in Acadia National Park, Maine.

▲ This is a historic painting of a Chippewa village.

Climate and terrain

Summers can be very hot and humid, while winters are usually cold and snowy. The terrain of the Northeast region is also very diverse. There are great forests, wide open fields, and tall mountains. There are also hills and valleys, waterways and wetlands. Some early Northeast Indians lived in the woodlands. Some lived along rivers and lakes. Others lived near the rocky cliffs and sandy beaches of the North Atlantic coastline.

How Did Early Northeast Indians Live?

Whether they lived in the forests or the mountains, beside the ocean or one of the Great Lakes, the early Northeast Indians shared the same basic needs of all people. For their families to survive, they had to have food, shelter, and clothing.

Homes and villages

Early Northeast Indians used two different kinds of shelters. Some preferred dome or cone-shaped homes called wigwams or wetus. They wove long grass or **reeds** or sheets of tree bark into mats. Twine or strips of leather were used to tie the mats together. These mats covered frames made of arched poles. This gave the wigwam or wetu its shape.

▲ The Algonquin Indians lived in bark covered wigwams like this one.

▲ The Iroquois people called themselves the Haudenosaunee, which means "People of the Longhouse."

Others built homes called longhouses. These homes looked like long, narrow barns. The frames were made of tree branches, covered with bark shingles. A longhouse was usually more than 18 feet (5 meters) wide. It could be anywhere from 40 to 200 feet (12 to 61 meters) long. There were doors on each end, and openings to let smoke from cooking fires escape. Several families lived in each longhouse, and several longhouses were built beside each other, to form a village.

Clothing of the early Northeast Indians

Early Northeast Indians made their own clothing from whatever materials were available to them. In hot weather, some wore lighter clothing made of green leaves, long grasses, and other plant fibers. In cooler weather, men wore shirts and leggings made of animal skins. They also wore breechcloths—clothing that resembled an apron, with front and back flaps that hung from a belt at the waist. In the winter, they bundled up in warm robes made of animal fur.

▲ This photograph taken in 1910 shows a Delaware Indian mother and daughter beautifully dressed in their finest clothes.

Women wore leggings and long dresses. Their dresses were often beautifully decorated with shells, paint, and porcupine quills. Later, they traded with European **settlers** for glass beads and ribbons, and cloth blankets that they used to make into hooded coats and capes.

Both men and women wore **moccasins**—soft shoes made of animal skin. On special occasions, they decorated their bodies with paint, piercings, and tattoos. They also wore jewelry made of shell or bone, and headdresses made of feathers.

Hairstyles

Hairstyles depended on what was popular in a particular **clan** or **tribe**. Women wore their hair long and loose or in braids, twists, or buns. Some men had long hair that they wore in braids. Others shaved their heads, or shaved part of their heads to create a specific style.

▲ Mohawk and Mohican (or Mahican) men wore their hair in **roaches**, shaving the sides of their heads to leave stiff columns of hair down the center. Today this hairstyle is called a "mohawk."

17

▲ From a birch bark canoe, this Algonquin man uses a spear to hunt and kill a moose.

Finding food

Early Northeast Indian men hunted for deer, moose, bear, elk, turkey, and rabbit. Other **prey** included otter, beaver, and mink. They used bows and arrows, spears and snares, or traps, to catch and kill these animals. They also fished in the lakes and rivers. Northeast Indians living near the ocean enjoyed oysters, clams, lobsters, shellfish, and even whales that had washed ashore.

The women gathered nuts and berries. In the spring, they harvested maple sap to make syrup and sugar. In the summer, they planted and grew corn, beans, pumpkins, and squash. They gathered the wild rice that grew along the banks of rivers, lakes, and streams. This rice was used to make many kinds of cereals, soups, and stews. It could be easily stored for the winter months when other foods were hard to find.

The Three Sisters

According to an Iroquois legend, a woman called Our Mother gave the world three gifts. These gifts were known as "The Three Sisters"—corn, squash, and beans. Corn grew from Our Mother's heart. Squash grew from her stomach. Beans grew from her fingers. Our Mother had two twin boys, Good Twin and Evil Twin. Good Twin taught the people how to use Our Mother's gifts to feed their families and keep them strong and healthy.

▲ This photograph shows an Ojibwe woman harvesting maple sap in the early 1900s.

Family life

Families usually consisted of one man, one woman, and their children. Each member of the family played an important role. Men were responsible for protecting and providing game. Women took care of the home. Although only men were chiefs and tribal council leaders, women's opinions were respected. In matters of war, men took the lead. When it came to issues that impacted the family, women often made the important decisions.

▲ This family of Menominee Americans huddle together outside their home on a cold winter's day.

Life of Early Northeast Indian Children

The birth of a baby was cause for celebration. Every child born into the tribe was considered a gift to the whole community. Everyone in the tribe was expected to help raise the children. Children were taught to show respect for others by listening to them. They also learned that arguing with or criticizing others was considered rude. Members of the tribe were expected to think before they spoke. They worked hard to care for one another.

The men taught the boys how to hunt and how to fight to protect the tribe from its enemies. Women taught the girls how to cook and sew and take care of their homes and farm. Everyone did their part to help the tribe survive, and those who had more wealth were expected to share with those who had less.

▲ Two young Menominee boys play with a turtle outside a birch bark wigwam.

Different languages

In one sense, each of the 50 northeastern tribes had their own language, their own **dialect** or accent. Words and phrases had a certain meaning to one tribe and a different meaning to another. However, a careful study of these languages reveals that they are actually very similar. They all fit into one of three larger language groups or families—the Algonquian family, the Iroquoian family, and the Sioux family. Members of the Sioux tribes were the first to move west, when the Europeans arrived in North America. Most of the remaining northeastern tribes are either Algonquin or Iroquois.

▲ The Algonquin tribes didn't have written languages. They used pictures and symbols instead of words to tell their family stories and record important events from their history.

Here are some words in English, Ojibwe (Algonquian), and Oneida (Iroquois):

English	Ojibwe	Oneida
man	inini	lukwé
woman	ikwe	yakukwé
dog	animosh	é:lhal
moon	dibik-Giizis	ohní:ta'
water	nibi	ohne:kánus
white	waabishki	Owískela'
yellow	ozaawi	Otsí:nkwala'
red	misko	Onikw htala'
black	makade	O'sw :ta'
eat	miijin or wiisini	í:laks
see	waabi	la:k he'
hear	noondam	lothu:té:
sing	nagamo	tehalihwákhwa'

What Were the Beliefs of the Early Northeast Indians?

Many early Northeast Indians believed that the world was full of spirit beings. Every rock and tree, every mountain and lake, and every animal had a spirit. All of the spirits were meant to live in harmony, coexisting peacefully together. According to their beliefs, there were also **supernatural** spirit beings that **inhabited** the sky and the Earth. These spirits often intervened, or got involved, in people's lives. They guided and protected the people by giving them wisdom and pointing them to the truth. Other Northeast Indians shared a deep faith in a Creator.

▲ A healer, or *Mide*, mixes plants, roots, and herbs to make special medicines to help cure others of their illnesses.

Dream Catchers

Dream catchers were made to trap and tangle up nightmares. Good dreams could then slip through the net, down the feathers, and into a person's head.

Healers

Some early Northeast Indians became part of the *Midewiwin* or Grand Medicine Society. These men and women were called *Mides*. They learned how to use plants and herbs to cure sickness. They carried medicine bundles, which were pouches filled with **sacred** objects that were thought to have special powers.

Visions and dreams

Early Northeast Indians often looked for spiritual guidance through visions and dreams. They believed that dreams could reveal all kinds of things about a person's heart and life. Many of the **descendants** of the Northeast Indians still practice this **traditional** faith today.

▲ This is a photograph of a dream catcher. The Ojibwe and the Huron believed dreams were a very important source of spiritual guidance.

Stories and legends

Mides often belonged to a secret society known as the False Face Society. They performed special healing rituals wearing carved wooden masks called False Faces. These healing rituals are still practiced today. The False Faces had deep-set eyes, crooked noses, and large mouths. These masks were worn to honor Old Broken Nose. According to myth, a stranger challenged the Creator to a contest to see who was the most powerful. As they were both sitting with their backs to a mountain, the Creator used his power to move the mountain closer to them. The stranger turned to see what the Creator was doing and smacked his face right into the mountain, crushing his nose. After losing the contest, Old Broken Nose promised the Creator that in the future, he would use his powers to heal hurting people.

There are many other interesting stories and legends that are a part of Northeast Indian **culture**. The Northeast Indians have stories about the creation of the world and the great flood.

▲ In some Algonquin stories, Glooscap is the Creator of the American Indian people. In others, he is their hero—a mighty warrior who rescues them from their enemies.

They also have stories that explain the origin of people, plants, and animals. Many of the main characters in their stories are animals—Master Rabbit, Otter, Partridge, Wolf, Wild Cat, and Bear. There are also stories about powerful giants, skillful hunters, brave warriors, and beautiful **maidens**.

▲ Diamond Brown is a story teller who shares American Indian legends at special ceremonies and events such as the Mohegan Park Indian Festival and Pow Wow in Ohio.

Celebrating life

Storytelling was an important way for early Northeast Indians to celebrate their culture and their way of life. Some of the best storytellers were women. They would often act out the stories as the tales were told. Most **tribes** had no written language, so their children learned their tribal and family histories by listening to older people tell stories about the past.

▲ This water drum is made from pieces of wood carefully fitted together and covered with animal hide. It has a special pot inside that can be filled with water. Changing the amount of water changes the tone or sound the drum makes.

Early Northeast Indian members also celebrated their beliefs in their art, music, and dance. Women sewed amazing patterns and designs on their clothing. Men carved fancy details onto their tools and their children's toys. They made their own musical instruments, including drums, rattles, and flutes.

Dances were performed as part of religious ceremonies. Each dance had its own special steps and movements. Children learned to do the dances by watching their parents and grandparents. Northeast Indians still perform these ceremonies and celebrations today.

Early Northeast Indians often had to fight for the survival of their families. Still, they found time to laugh and play. People enjoyed all kinds of games. They ran races, threw arrows at targets, and hid special objects for others to find. They also played stick and ball games similar to hockey or **lacrosse**.

◄ These are game sticks made by members of the Menominee Nation.

When Did Northeast Indians First Meet Europeans?

In 1587 Sir Walter Raleigh tried to establish a **colony** for England in Roanoke, Virginia. Several Algonquin **tribes** were already living in the area.

Members of the Powhatan **Confederacy** first met the English in 1607, when **settlers** built a fort in Jamestown, Virginia. At the same time, members of the Iroquois Confederacy found French explorers on their lands around the Great Lakes. Some Spanish explorers were there, too, according to John Smith.

In 1621, the Wampanoag Indians began a friendship with the settlers at the Plymouth Plantation in Massachusetts.

BIOGRAPHY

Pocahontas

Pocahontas was the daughter of Chief Powhatan. Powhatan had captured explorer Captain John Smith and was about to execute (kill) him. Pocahontas begged her father to spare his life. Later Pocahontas became friends with the English settlers living in Jamestown. She married an Englishman, John Rolfe, and together they had a son named Thomas.

▲ Pocahontas interfered to stop her father from executing John Smith.

▲ Captain John Smith arrived at the Jamestown fort in the colony of Virginia in 1607.

Squanto

Squanto was a Patuxet Indian who helped the settlers survive their first winter in the New World. He taught them how to plant the crops that grew best in North American soil. He showed them the best places to catch fish and eels. The settlers were grateful for his friendship. They called him a "gift from God."

How Did the Life of Northeast Indians Change?

The Europeans brought with them all kinds of new things that the Northeast Indians had never seen before. They brought new technology, new weapons (like guns), new tools, fabrics, and other household items. The Northeast Indians found that the **settlers** were anxious to trade these items for things they needed. The settlers needed food. They wanted land and lumber. They also wanted animal furs that they could send back to Europe and sell for a lot of money.

▶ For a time, trade with Europeans made the Northeast Indians some of the wealthiest and most prosperous people.

Unfortunately, the Europeans also brought with them sickness and disease. These illnesses wiped out entire **tribes** and **nations**. There were also constant conflicts and misunderstandings between Indians and the settlers. Their disagreements often led to war. Then there were the wars between the settlers. The English, French, and Spanish often fought for control of the North American **continent**. Sometimes the Northeast Indians took sides and fought alongside the settlers against other settlers and other tribes.

ART AND CULTURE

Wampum

The Iroquois treasured *wampum*—special white and purple beads made from shells. They believed that strings of these beads could bring comfort and healing to suffering people. The beads were also used to make belts and jewelry that were worn in **sacred** ceremonies. When European traders realized how much the Northeast Indians valued wampum, they started making the beads in large quantities.

▲ Disagreements over trade led to conflict—not only between the Northeast Indians and the settlers—but between rival tribes fighting for control of territory and trading rights.

Learning to live together

The Northeast Indians taught the European settlers many things. They showed the newcomers how to plant and harvest a wide variety of the fruits and vegetables that grew in North American soil. They knew how to make cotton and tobacco crops grow successfully. The Northeast Indians had also discovered plants that had medicinal (healing) properties. Indian labor helped build the "New World." Their hard work in the fur trade made many European nations wealthy.

◄ Jane Johnston Schoolcraft was the daughter of an Ojibwe woman and a Scots-Irish fur trader. She wrote beautiful poems about her love of nature, faith, and family.

◄ The first Bible ever printed in America was an Algonquin Language Bible, created by **missionary** John Eliot in 1663.

Over time, the Algonquin and Iroquois tribes adapted some European **customs** and **culture**, and made them part of their own. They used the new weapons, tools, and technology to improve their lives. Many Northeast Indians learned to speak English, French, or Spanish. They also learned to read and write. This helped them create a written record of their own languages, cultures, and histories.

Missionaries

Christian missionaries came to share their faith with the Northeast Indians. Many Northeast Indians became Christians. Others took Christian teachings and combined them with their own **traditional** faith to create a blended religion that is still practiced by some Northeast Indians today.

Why Did the Northeast Indians Lose Their Lands?

For hundreds of years, there had been **tension** between Northeast Indians and the European **settlers** who had come to North America. Although at times they lived in peace, more often they were at war. They fought over who owned the land, who had the right to live there, and whose laws and **customs** should be obeyed. The Northeast Indians were outnumbered. Although they fought back fiercely, they could not hold onto their lands.

▲ This engraving shows Northeast Indians attacking a village in Massachusetts during King Philip's War in 1675.

Moving to the reservations

In the 1800s, the U. S. government passed laws forcing all American Indians to move onto **reservations**. These were specific areas of land set aside for them. Many of the Northeast Indians had already lost their lands—unofficially—centuries earlier. Since the first explorers, thousands of people had moved in and forced them out. Some **tribes** had gone north into Canada or west across the Mississippi River. Others were wiped out by **famine**, disease, and war. Those who were left had to make a choice. They could live alongside the new settlers and observe their laws and customs, or they could move onto reservations and try to keep their **traditional** life.

BIOGRAPHY

A Century of Dishonor

In 1881 Helen Hunt Jackson (1830-1855) published a book called *A Century of Dishonor*, exposing the mistreatment of American Indians. She sent copies to every member of Congress to remind them of their responsibility for the suffering of thousands of people.

◀ Helen Hunt Jackson brought attention to the mistreatment of American Indians by the U.S. government.

Where Are the Northeast Indians Today?

Today many **descendants** of the Northeast Indians live in the United States and Canada. Some choose to live on Indian **reservations** such as the Penobscot Reservation in Maine and the Mashantucket Pequot Reservation in Connecticut. Most, however, choose to make their homes in towns and cities among people of all different races and **cultures**. There are more Northeast Indians living in New York and Michigan than in any other Northeastern states.

In many ways, they live just like other Americans. They work as teachers, doctors, lawyers, and engineers. Some are artists, athletes, actors, and entertainers. Others work in farming or fishing. Northeast Indians operate campgrounds and tourist attractions. They own restaurants, hotels, and other businesses.

▲ Brett and Drew Bucktooth and their father take a break from competition at an Iroquois Nationals **lacrosse** tournament. Their team plays all over the world, representing the Iroquois **Nation** in international competition.

While living their modern lives, however, these American Indians try to **preserve** the history and culture of their **ancestors**. They want their children to understand where they have come from and what it means to be a Northeast Indian. Parents and grandparents work especially hard to pass on these traditions to the next **generation**.

▲ It is important to teach young Northeast Indians the languages that their grandparents and great-grandparents used to speak. Otherwise, these languages will soon become endangered or even **extinct**—and a part of their culture will be lost forever.

Staying connected

There are many books, magazines, and newspapers that celebrate the Northeast Indian way of life. Museums and cultural centers display historical **artifacts**. They house samples of **traditional** fine arts, basketry, pottery, tools, instruments, jewelry, and clothing. New technology is also making it possible for Northeast Indians to preserve their past. Websites and online groups help them connect with one another to share their history and culture with the world.

Festivals and celebrations

Each year, hundreds of Northeast Indians gather at Indian festivals across the country. They perform ceremonial songs and dances. They share traditional arts and crafts and recipes. Rodeos and parades are often part of the festivities. By participating in these events, the American Indian peoples celebrate their past, present, and future.

▲ This birch bark wigwam is one of many important artifacts on display at the Menominee Indian Museum in Green Bay, Wisconsin. Members of the Menominee tribes are working to create a virtual museum online, so that people all over the world can learn more about the Menominee history and culture by viewing photographs of the exhibits.

▲ This photograph shows an American Indian man dressed in traditional clothing at a cultural celebration at the National Museum of the American Indian in Washington, D.C.

Timeline

1400s   The Five Great Tribes—Cayuga, Mohawk, Oneida, Onondaga, and Seneca—form the Iroquois **Confederacy**, also known as the Iroquois League of Five **Nations**.

1492   Explorer Christopher Columbus becomes the first European to "discover" the New World.

1607   Just outside of Jamestown, Virginia, Captain John Smith is captured by Chief Powhatan of the Powhatan tribe, and saved from death by the chief's daughter, Pocahontas.

1616   A smallpox epidemic nearly wipes out the American Indian population in New England.

1634   More than 600 Pequot Indians are killed in the Pequot War, which began as a trade dispute between the Pequot and the English and Dutch **settlers** and their American Indian allies (the Mohegan and the Narragansett).

1643   The Mohawk and Seneca attack the Huron in a series of conflicts over trade known as the Beaver Wars.

1675   King Philip's War costs the lives of 600 colonists and 3,000 American Indians in New England.

1754   Some Northeast Indians join the French in a losing battle against the British in the French and Indian Wars.

1758   The first Indian **Reservation** in North America is established by the New Jersey Colonial Assembly.

1763   Ottawa Indians attack British forts in a conflict called Pontiac's Rebellion.

1776 Some Northeast Indians ally with the British in a losing battle against the colonists during the American Revolution.

1881 Helen Hunt Jackson publishes a book called *A Century of Dishonor*, exposing the mistreatment of American Indians by the U.S. government.

1924 The Indian Citizenship Act extends citizenship and voting rights to all American Indians. (Not all are in favor of this.)

1934 The Indian Reorganization Act returns American Indians' authority to self-govern and reverses some of the unfair government policies of the past.

1968 The American Indian Movement (AIM) organizes protests against the unfair treatment of and calls on the government to keep its promises to the people.

1990 Congress passes the Native American Languages Act, "to **preserve**, protect, and promote the rights and freedoms of all Native Americans to use, practice and develop Native American languages."

1990 On August 3, President George H. W. Bush proclaims the first National American Indian Heritage Month. President Clinton affirms this special designation in November of 1996.

2004 The National Museum of the American Indian is established on the National Mall in Washington, DC.

Glossary

ancestor family member that lived a long time ago; great-grandparents, great great-grandparents, and so on

anthropologist scientist who studies the beliefs and ways of life of different people

artifact object belonging to or used by people of the past

characteristic something that makes a person special or different from others

clan large group of families that are related to each other

colony distant territory belonging to or under the control of another nation; group of people living in one of these territories

confederacy group of people united by a common goal or cause

continent one of the seven large land masses of the Earth, including Asia, Africa, Europe, North America, South America, Australia, and Antarctica

culture a group's beliefs, traditions, and way of life

custom usual way of doing things for a particular group of people

descendant children, grandchildren, great-grandchildren, and so on

dialect way a language is spoken by a particular group of people

extinct something that has died out or no longer exists

famine great shortage of food

generation group of people born during a certain time

Great Law system of government created by the nations of the Iroquois confederacy

Ice Age period of time thousands of years ago, when Earth's climate was much colder and entire regions were covered by glaciers

inhabit live or dwell in

lacrosse game played on a field, using nets on sticks to catch, throw, or carry a ball

maiden young, unmarried woman

missionary person who travels to other places to share his or her faith and do good works

moccasin soft shoe made of animal skin

nation group of people who live in the same part of the world and share the same language, customs, and government

natural resource substance found in nature that has many important uses

preserve keep safe

prey animal that is hunted for food

prophet spiritual guide or leader

reed tall, slender grass

reservation area of land set aside by the U.S. government as a place for American Indians to live

sacred holy; having to do with religion; set apart

settler person who moves to a new place and builds a home there

supernatural out of the ordinary, beyond the laws of nature

tension unfriendliness between groups of people

terrain ground or land

traditional based on customs handed down one generation to another

tribe group of people who are related to each other and share the same laws, customs, and beliefs

Find Out More

Books

Adil, Janeen R. *The Northeast Indians: Daily Life in the 1500s*. Mankato, Minn.: Capstone Press, 2006.

Bruchac, Joseph. *Squanto's Journey: The Story of the First Thanksgiving*. San Diego, Calif.: Harcourt, 2007.

Murdoch, David S. *North American Indian*. New York: DK Eyewitness Books, 2005.

Silver, Donald M. and Patricia J. Wynne. *Easy Make and Learn Projects: Northeast Indians*. New York: Scholastic, 2005.

Websites

Native American Facts for Kids
www.native-languages.org/kids.htm
This website provides simple information about American Indians in an easy-to-read question and answer format.

First People of America and Canada
www.firstpeople.us/
This is an educational site full of great information about American Indians and members of the First Nations of Canada.

DVDs

500 Nations. Directed by Jack Leustig. Warner Home Video, 2004.

A History of American Indian Achievement. Directed by Ron Meyer. Ambrose Video, 2008.

We Shall Remain: America Through Native Eyes. Directed by Chris Eyre and Sharon Grimberg. PBS, 2009.

Places to visit

The National Museum of the American Indian
Fourth Street and Independence Avenue SW
Washington, D.C.
www.nmai.si.edu/

The George Gustav Heye Center
One Bowling Green
New York, NY
www.nmai.si.edu/subpage.cfm?subpage=visitor&second=ny

Museum of Indian Culture
Allentown, PA
www.lenape.org/

Further research

What did you find to be the most interesting about the Northeast Indians?
How does life for these people compare to the way American Indians live
today in other regions? You can find out much more by visiting your local
library or searching online.

Index